HEELING
YOUR INNER DOG

Heeling Your
INNER
NER
DOG

A Self-Whelp Book

ILLUSTRATIONS BY

Danny Shanahan

NICOLE GREGORY
and JUDITH STONE

TIMES BOOKS

RANDOM HOUSE

All rights reserved under International and Pan-American Copyright Conventions. Published in the United States by Times Books, a division of Random House, Inc., New York, and simultaneously in Canada by Random House of Canada Limited, Toronto.

Grateful acknowledgment is made to the following for permission to reprint previously published material:

Doubleday, a division of Bantam Doubleday Dell Publishing Group, Inc.: Illustration composed of excerpts from six dance-step diagrams from *The Complete Book of Ballroom Dancing* by Richard M. Stephenson and Joseph Iaccarino. Copyright © 1980 by Richard M. Stephenson and Joseph Iaccarino. Reprinted by permission of Doubleday, a division of Bantam Doubleday Dell Publishing Group, Inc.

Penguin Books USA Inc.: Illustration of a man and a woman from *A Healthy Body* by The Diamond Group. Copyright © 1981 by Diagram Visual Information Ltd. Reprinted by permission of New American Library, a division of Penguin Books USA Inc.

Reader's Digest Books: Illustration of a toilet pump from *Reader's Digest Complete Do-It-Yourself Manual*. Copyright © 1973 by The Reader's Digest Association, Inc. Reprinted by permission.

Library of Congress Cataloging-in-Publication Data

Gregory, Nicole.
Heeling your inner dog : a self-whelp book / Nicole Gregory and Judith Stone. — 1st ed.
p.   cm.
ISBN 0-8129-2139-9
1. Dogs—Humor.   2. Inner child—Humor.
3. Self-actualization (Psychology)—Humor.
4. Psychotherapy—Humor.   I. Stone, Judith.
II. Title.
PN6231.D68G74   1993
818'.5402—dc20   92-56850

BOOK DESIGN BY CATHRYN S. AISON

Manufactured in the United States of America

9   8   7   6   5   4   3   2

FIRST EDITION

932628

TO DANIEL TAMM,
WHO MAKES ME THE LUCKY DOG I AM TODAY
—N.G.

TO DENNIS ANDERSEN
AND HIS INNER DOG POKEY
—J.S.

ACKNOWLEDGMENTS

Our thanks to Jim Anderson, Judith Wederholt Coyne, Dennis Dalrymple, Rosemary Ellis, Jarrod Fischer, Zachary Fischer, Karen Glenn, the Gregory family, Margaret Jaworski, Stuart Krichevsky, Tom Passavant, Richard Pine, Andrew Postman, Jamie Raab, Elizabeth Rapoport and her jolly colleagues at Times Books, Kathy Rich, Saundra Schwartz, Teresa Shelley, the Stone family, Marcia Tamm, and Louie von Schluie.

CONTENTS

HEELING
YOUR INNER DOG

A NEW LEASH
ON LIFE

How the Movement Was Born

Five years ago, we were the most respected marriage counselors in America, famous for saving seemingly doomed relationships. Our book *Saving the Seemingly Doomed Relationship* was a national best-seller.

What the world didn't know was that America's favorite shrinks, George and Harriet Halbleib, were growing—no, hurtling—in opposite directions. Our own marriage was in serious trouble.

Harriet's quest for self took her East; she joined a Tibetan singing-bowl ensemble and studied hatha-yoga. George went West, to a series of Native American drumming weekends. We reconciled briefly after George nearly electrocuted himself trying to use a cellular phone in a sweat lodge.

But soon we were out of sync again. George went inner with biofeedback; Harriet went outer with fire-walking. George went yin, Harriet went yang. George said "potato," Harriet said "potahto." George said "tipi," Harriet said "teepee." And the only time we spoke to each other was when we counseled other couples.

Then came the worst fight of our lives. It was the night before Harriet was scheduled to leave for Goddess Camp and George for a men's Restore Your Positive Fierceness retreat. Both of us were reeling from deep betrayals. Harriet had discovered her aroma therapist was charging a fortune for imported essential oils that were actually scraped from the fragrance strips in magazine ads and mixed with seltzer. George was devastated when Bob Vila left "This Old House" to do Sears commercials. We were dry tinder waiting for a spark. The flash point: we each wanted to take the Saab.

"I don't give a rat's ass if you want to join a Ty-D-Bol ensemble or do Hiawatha-yoga," George snapped, "or sit around with a bunch of broads in nighties summoning the goddess Aspartame." He was fairly howling. "But you're taking the Hyundai!"

Harriet was enraged beyond howling. She bit George on the leg.

That was the jolt we needed.

We canceled our trips and sat up all night talking. What had happened when George howled and Harriet snapped? What deep, hidden realm of the psyche had we tapped? The world knew about the Inner Child. It was about to discover the Inner Child's best friend: the Inner Dog.

The Inner Dog Movement is born.

YOUR K-9 CORE:

Defining the Inner Dog

What is the Inner Dog? It is the innate core of joy, creativity, courage, and exuberant, unrepentant slobbering living deep within each of us. It is the hidden, happy, healthy primal self.

For all of us, the internal canine starts life as *Wonder Dog*—good, trusting, playful, ready to lick the world. Wonder Dog is present when we celebrate, dance, love, laugh with friends, or pee on a hydrant.

But in most of us Wonder Dog's woof is warped by shame-based parenting, toxic grandparenting, punitive aunting, neglectful uncling, and mudslinging siblinging. We're soon at the mercy of *Hang Dog*, the wounded hound within, tail permanently between its legs, perpetually in the doghouse.

If you're like most people, you wouldn't know your Inner Dog if it bit you on the butt. Nevertheless, it is probably screwing you up big-time. Learn to recognize the ten warning signs of Inner Dog damage:

🐾 Occasional snacking.

🐾 Holiday depression.

🐾 Periodic water retention.

🐾 Awakening with an erection (men only).

🐾 A mild rash.

🐾 The inability to remember the difference between Steely Dan and Steeleye Span.

🐾 Putting off doing your income tax.

🐾 Mange.

🐾 Frequent sighing.

🐾 A wart or mole that suddenly assumes the shape of the Mercedes-Benz logo.

The first step in reclaiming and heeling your Inner Dog is confronting it.

ARE YOU
A SICK PUP?

A *Questionnaire*

Since a quarter past the dawn of time, humankind has been attempting to reduce the psyche to its component parts. Perhaps that's why there's so little mental health today.

In the late nineteenth century Sigmund Freud divided the mind into the ego (the rational self), the superego (the conscience), and the id (primal, uncontrollable urges such as sex, looking into a Kleenex after you blow your nose, putting your tongue in the hole left by a missing tooth, or saying "Peep!" after your father says "One more peep out of you and you'll be sorry").

Freud's disciple, the Swiss psychologist Carl Jung, added to the master's schema the notion of a collective unconscious, a part of the psyche that retains and transmits the common psychological inheritance of mankind. He also coined the terms *extrovert*, *introvert*, and *nutbag*.

Later, the founder of Transactional Analysis, Eric Berne, preferred yet another mental breakdown: child, adult, and parent. Dr. Jean-Claude Pep, the noted psychiatrist and automotive-parts magnate, followed nearly the same model but called the components Manny, Moe, and Jack.

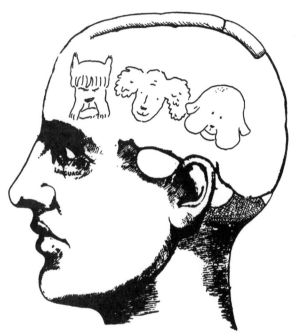

*Dr. Fritz Dreistoogen divided the psyche
into three parts.*

(Curiously, Pep's Austrian rival, Dr. Fritz Drei-stoogen, echoed the work of his nemesis by segmenting the psyche into three parts designated Larry, Moe, and Curly. For a detailed study of the importance of both Pep's and Dreistoogen's Moe mode in psychological rebirth and recovery, see our book *Moe Better Blues: A Poke in the Eye from the Wise Guy Within.*)

Inner Dog theory is a synthesis of all that came before it, and then some. The sooner you complete the following questionnaire, the sooner Inner Dog theory can work for you.

1. I am the adult child of former children.

YES _____   NO _____

2. I tend to confuse pity with love,
and Upton Sinclair with Sinclair Lewis.

YES _____   NO _____

3. I was always teacher's pet.

YES _____   NO _____

4. Squirrels interest me strangely.

YES _____   NO _____

5. When I saw *Cats*, I felt the urge to rush the stage.

YES _____   NO _____

6. My two favorite colors are Old Rose and Old Yeller.

YES _____   NO _____

7. I'm easy—I'll roll over for anyone.

YES _____   NO _____

8. One crack of thunder and I'm under the bed.

YES _____   NO _____

9. I like to drive with my head out the window.

YES _____ NO _____

10. I'm most loyal to someone who feeds me,
tells me I'm good, and clips my toenails.

YES _____ NO _____

11. I'm a people pleaser.

YES _____ NO _____

12. I'm a people eater.

YES _____ NO _____

13. I drool over my friends' good fortune.

YES _____ NO _____

14. I drool over my friends.

YES _____ NO _____

15. I have trouble making decisions;
I respond well to commands.

YES _____ NO _____

16. Which statement best matches what you feel:

    ____ Why shouldn't I tip over garbage cans? If I didn't, someone else would.

    ____ If I don't do tricks, no one will like me.

    ____ Why bother to carry a tennis ball in my mouth? No one's going to throw it for me anyway.

    ____ I have to beg for whatever scraps I can get.

SCORING: If you answered yes to any question above, your Inner Dog is wounded, and you need professional help. If you answered no to any question above, you are in deep denial and need professional help.

In either case, this book—a distillation of what we[*] teach at our famous Inner Dog Workshops—will help you get in touch with and transform your Inner Dog. Keep a copy by your bedside and another in the bathroom, near the Victoria's Secret catalog; carry a copy with you. Dip into it daily. If you're short on time, simply skim the aphorisms that we think of as soulchow and brain kibble for the Inner Dog—tender, meaty nuggets of wisdom served up in a rich gravy of experience.

---

[*]We, George and Harriet, refer to ourselves throughout the book as both "we" and "us"—a tribute to our newfound commitment to togetherness—and as "George," "Harriet," "he," and "she," as an acknowledgment of our separate uniqueness.

If you think owning your feelings is hard, try renting them.

THE PAWS
THAT REFRESH

Inside an Inner Dog Workshop

N'anceigh R. is a high-fashion model. You'd know her face instantly. It would take you much, much longer to know her pain.

N'anceigh is afraid she doesn't deserve her good fortune. She hides her fear behind endless discussions of under-eye concealer, cellulite creams, and other possible spellings of her name. It hurts when people call her an airhead. That's why she's acting like an Airedale.

Yes. Tonight N'anceigh is down on all fours, baying like a bitch in heat. And the men and women surrounding her cheer and applaud. This is what happens so often at a weekend-long Halbleib Inner Dog workshop.

Two hundred people, divided into "litters" of five, jam the Albert Payson Terhune Room of the Matoon, Illinois, Holiday Inn this particular Sunday. Many clutch rubber balls, squeaky toys, bones sucked bald. In one group Jessica S. ecstatically scratches for fleas. Over in the corner, Jason P. is unashamedly gnawing on a Reebok, tears streaming down his face. Fellow participants pat his head and scratch his stomach. "Good boy!" they say. " 'Atta pooch!" He has found, finally, the freedom and affirmation denied him in his youth. He has found his Inner Dog.

Kyle and his Inner Dog, Foofy.

As his "littermates" yip softly, Kyle G. reads a fax that his Inner Dog, whom he's named Foofy, would like to send to his father and mother:

"I always felt so alone. You wormed me and walked me, but you never really made me feel I mattered." Kyle/Foofy begins to whimper. "All you cared about was whether the neighbors admired my coat and—"

He can't go on and begins to yowl. The group joins in. Then they praise Kyle for his bravery, and give him—or, rather, the liberated Foofy once locked within him—the stroking he's been waiting for all his life.

For years, without even being aware of it, Kyle and N'anceigh had been ruled by shame-based Hang Dog.

You know Hang Dog's in charge when you put yourself down, choose unhappiness, get stuck in bad relationships, pout, manipulate, throw tantrums, or chew on your mate's slippers. Hang Dog is the source of all obsessive, compulsive, addictive, and acting-out behavior. When you told your fifth-grade teacher that the dog ate your homework, you were not technically lying.

Through a process called Species Regression (Reg. Penna. Dept. Agr.), Halbleib workshop participants like Kyle and N'anceigh can, with astonishing speed, relive their early shame, detoxify it, deodorize it, then reclaim and embrace the Inner Dog. We have known participants to transform their lives *before we even deposit their check*!

And it's no temporary fix but a change guaranteed to last longer than the next Italian government. As N'anceigh put it, "I'm like a new person, and I've been like a new person for like a month!"

We begin Species Regression by describing the normal dependency needs of the inner pup—for safety, love, and approval, and for acknowledgment of what some experts call our I-AM-NESS but we think is more accurately termed our HEY-WHAT-AM-I-CHOPPED-LIVER?-NESS.

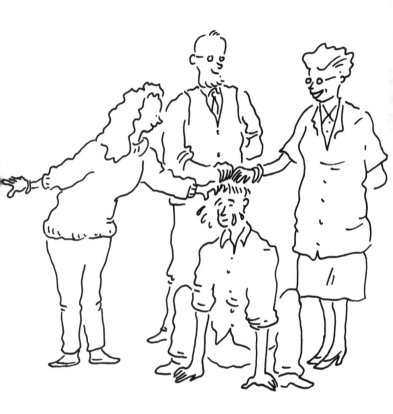

The Halbleibs help restore Jason's
HEY-WHAT-AM-I-CHOPPED-LIVER?-NESS.

Then we explain what happens if those needs are not met. If your caretaker withheld the rawhide pork chop of unconditional love and instead whacked you with the rolled-up newspaper of disapproval, you learned that you're not enough. You felt shamed, you felt double shamed, you felt everybody knew your name—but you. You learned that you could not trust your caretakers; you grew up without models of healthy emotional expression.

We offer exercises that provide those models, thus freeing your wounded Inner Dog from the cruel pound of repression. First, we have each litter observe an actual dog (provided for a small materials fee). Though the Inner Dog concept is, of course, metaphorical, it helps to see the

A cat is provided for a small materials fee.

canine qualities we wish to emulate played out: enthusiasm, energy, steadfastness, loyalty, leg-humping. Then, as a preliminary liberating exercise, each group chases a live cat (available for a small materials fee). Participants start out feeling sheepish, but soon feel doggish—and free. (Be assured that the cat's uniqueness and integrity are honored and protected at all times.)

But our system isn't about self-indulgence. It's about finding the discipline that's the only real road to release. Kyle, N'anceigh, and the others learn to come when they call themselves. They become helpless in order to help themselves; they lose control in order to gain control.

You say our advice sounds inconsistent and contradictory? Good for you for noticing. *You* are the expert on your life, not us. We're just the ones getting paid up front.

Later, over white wine and Liv-a-Snaps, N'anceigh, Kyle, Jessica, Jason, and so many others express relief and joy at getting in touch with their Inner Dogs. Many are working other programs that are perfectly complemented by Inner Dog material. N'anceigh, for example, has been a longtime member of Survivors of Bad Haircuts, but that alone hasn't been enough to help her. Jason had sought solace, unsuccessfully, by joining both Adult Children of Teamsters and Adult Grandchildren of Cheek-Pinching Bubbes. Others have reported that Inner Dog work has helped speed their progress in ManTongue, the gay stutterers' support group, or WomanFoot, the arch-support group.

But they weren't truly transformed until they unleashed their Inner Dogs and became the nurturing masters they never had, powerful enough to rebirth, housebreak, and retrain themselves.

They had to whelp themselves to help themselves. They had to heel themselves to heal themselves.

Now you can do the same, using the exercises in this book. You'll find them in the section called "New Tricks" at the end of each chapter.

*You must heel yourself
to heal yourself.*

NEW TRICKS

You're em*barking* on an exciting journey (italics ours, but available for a small materials fee). Here's the equipment you'll need:

paper	wet ceramic clay
scissors	magazines for cutting
rock	and pasting
glue	1 tablespoon minced
fingerpaints	shallots
crayons	½ cup dry white vermouth
string	1 tablespoon lemon juice
backhoe	1 tablespoon prepared
hydrolized collagen	Dijon-style mustard
glitter	salt and pepper to taste
	AMP-Isostearol

1. Paper training:
   Drawing and drawing out your inner dog

The best way to allow your Inner Dog to begin communicating with you is nonverbally. On paper, with clay, or using the medium of your choice, create a portrait of your Inner Dog as you imagine it. Include favorite toys, significant others, insignificant others, etc. Don't censor.

HINT: You'll access your unconscious more easily if you hold the pen, paintbrush, or soldering iron between your teeth as you create. At the very least, use your non-dominant hand.

2. *Getting in touch with your inner dog*

Study the portrait carefully, then close your eyes.

🐾 Prepare to banish your inner critical master. Say out loud, "I banish my inner critical master."

🐾 Give your Inner Dog permission to come out and play. Say out loud, "I give my Inner Dog permission to come out and play."

🐾 Imagine a safe, beautiful place where you and your Inner Dog, in whatever form it takes, can get together. (We suggest Just Three Guys from Bucharest, a restaurant and lounge with locations in most major metropolitan areas; mention the Halbleibs and your Inner Dog dines free!)

🐾 Sit quietly and let your Inner Dog come to you. It may be reluctant; you may have to lure it with meat or meat by-products, provocative pictures of mail carriers, cash prizes, or factory-to-dealer incentives (some restrictions apply). If none of this works, you may have to subpoena your Inner Dog.

3. *Chewing the fat with your inner dog*

Write out a dialogue with your Inner Dog, using your dominant hand when you are speaking and your nondominant hand when your Inner Dog is responding (or hold the pen in your mouth). Start by asking your Inner Dog what it needs from you in order to feel cared for. Then ask whatever question pops into your head: its name, its age, its opinion on the designated-hitter rule, whether it prefers smooth to chunky. Ask if there's anything else it wants to tell you.

This is precisely the method George and Harriet Halbleib used to get in touch with their Inner Dogs, Thurston and Lovey Howl.

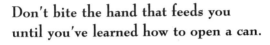

Don't bite the hand that feeds you until you've learned how to open a can.

Try not to judge your dog. Remember: *You were born best of breed.* Here's an example of a dialogue that got off to a less than promising start; the client, Yosemite S., had a defense system that would have made the Joint Chiefs of Staff olive drab with envy.

INNER DOG: *I'm scared and hurt.*

YOSEMITE S.: You must have me confused with someone who gives a shit.

ID: *I need you to take care of me.*

YS: Well, you lose, jerk-off.

ID: *Is that my name? Jerk-off? Thank you for telling me.*

YS: Let's get this straight; I only came to this workshop because it was a condition of my probation.

Clearly, a part of Yosemite S. was crying out for nurturing, but his inner ears were clogged with the wax of denial.

Baseball near-great Bob "Death to Flying Things" F., a utility infielder who recently became a free agent, wanted to consult his Inner Dog about his next career move. Self-help of any kind was new to him, although he had used Chaw-Enders to give up pouch tobacco. He was unsure about who should initiate the dialogue.

BOB F.: Okay, who's on first?

INNER DOG: *Yes.*

BF: What?

ID: *No, What's on second.*

BF: Are you the fellow who knows all the players?

ID: *Why, certainly.*

BF: Then who's on first?

ID: *Yes.*

We intervened at this point and suggested that a better approach might be to ask the Inner Dog about its turn-ons and turn-offs. With a little coaching, Bob got the hang of Inner Dog work and soon realized he was really a shame-based baseman. His interpersonal skills improved, but his game still sucked.

Often people learn surprising things about themselves from these dialogues. J.W., a sadistic border patrolman from Laredo, Texas, discovered that his Inner Dog is a bright, sensitive Mexican Hairless named Chuy who's looking for a better way of life, and that his persecution of illegal aliens sprang from his own feelings of illegitimacy and alienation.

HINT: It's important that your Inner Dog be protected. Don't discuss your dialogues with people who are not welcoming to who you truly are, people who are out of touch with their own Inner Dogs, or people who are in denial (nearly everyone) since they're likely to make fun of you because they're threatened.

Confide only in someone you know is trustworthy—a priest, a parole officer, a hair colorist, a reiki therapist, a past-life regresser, or Salman Rushdie's advance man. Or don't discuss your Inner Dog Work at all; try journaling instead of conversationaling.

ANOTHER HINT: A discreet way to find out whether someone has done Inner Dog Work is to ask, "Are you a friend of George and Harriet's?" To discover whether a social event will be attended by others involved in Inner Dog Work, ask the host or hostess, "Should I wear my Pucci?"

4. *Listen to yourself*

Analyze closely the words you use to describe yourself:

🐾 "I have a *dis-ease*." You aren't at ease with yourself.

🐾 "I'm *dis-couraged*." Naturally! Your innate courage has been spanked out of you.

🐾 "I'm *dis-gusted*." Of course! Your God-given gust disappeared the first time your parents took the wind out of your sails.

- "I'm *con-fused*." Your identity is so *fused with* that of your parents that you can't make good decisions.

Perhaps you're even ready to commit *mans-laughter* or see a *the-rapist* to improve your *self-dis-cipli-ne*.

We will restore you to ease and courage and gust and separateness. You say you're drowning in neuroses? Well, we will teach you to see them as just that: *neu-roses*, the buds that were nipped and now have a chance to bloom again. We are committed to total canine wellness. In fact, we're probably the only celebrity therapists who *don't* want rabid fans!

I'd rather be dogmatic than catatonic.

WHERE THE BONES
ARE BURIED

How Early Hurt Still Hounds You

Mental-health profession-
als estimate that 95 percent of us grow up in dysfunctional
families. Mental-health amateurs put the number even
higher.❦

You may be saying to yourself, "So why not just lower
the curve?" That sort of remark is typical of those not yet
reacquainted with their Inner Dog and, we might add,
explains why the Japanese invented the dancing Coke can
before we did.

Leo Tolstoy was very close to the mark when he began
Anna Karenina—a co-dependency† poster girl if there ever

❦If you need any sign that the nation hungers for guidance in this area,
know that Disney World plans to add a new attraction, the Swiss
Dysfunctional Family Robinson Tree House, where visitors will be
encouraged to make as many therapeutic interventions as they wish.

†You've probably heard of co-dependency. Some of us form relationships
with the Inner Dog–impaired, we enable them—that is, allow them to
go on doing bad things—and then stick with them even if the relationship
is a damaging one. Other famous co-dependents include Tom and Jerry,
Ben and Jerry, and Jerry and Mick.

was one—in this way (as rendered in the new Leo Busca-glia translation): "Functional families are all alike; every dysfunctional family is dysfunctional in its own way."

But there *are* certain characteristics that define a dys-functional family. It is one in which the child's needs are not met, in which parents make such counternurturant and toxic remarks as:

🐾 "That's a good way to lose an eye."

🐾 "Stop crying or I'll give you something to cry about."

Typical toxic parenting: "You'd look so much nicer with your hair off your face."

🐾 "I don't care what all the other mothers are doing."

🐾 "You should have thought of that before we left."

🐾 "You'd look so much nicer with your hair off your face."

A dysfunctional family is one in which a child is not accepted for who she or he is. *The greatest wound any of us can suffer is the rejection of our authentic Inner Dog.* Maybe our parents wanted a pointer but got a setter; maybe they've never forgiven us for being born a Doberman instead of the poodle they'd longed for. We sensed their disappointment early in life and felt ashamed; we weren't enough. We fell prey to Hang Dog.

Paradoxically, a dysfunctional family is also one in which parents pay *too much* attention to a child's needs, denying the child a chance to develop a sense of potent selfhood and virtually ensuring that he or she grows up with engulfment issues and intimacy problems.

If we don't get our needs met—or if we get them met too enthusiastically; if we aren't accepted as children—or if we're too easily accepted—our healthy ego, our WHAT-AM-I-CHOPPED-LIVER?-NESS is damaged.

Furthermore, our dissatisfied, unloved, unhousebroken Inner Dog continues to crave care, shut away though it is. The only way it can get attention is to sabotage our happiness, screw up our adult relationships, turn us into harridans, bullies, addicts, materialists, control freaks, out-of-control freaks.

We'd like you to hear from an Inner Dog workshop

graduate who was the epitome of parentally induced Hang Dogness.

"Hi, I'm Josef K.," he began on the first evening he spoke, "and I'm powerless over my own fate, the fate of nations, and other people's annoying cheerful moods.

"My father used to bug me for being too paranoid. 'Relax, Josef, you big goof!' he'd say. 'Those Soviet tanks are here in Prague on maneuvers.' 'For God's sake, Josef, next you'll be telling me that Nixon has an enemies list.' 'Don't be silly, Josef. What could be dangerous about a Ford Pinto?'

"He discounted anything I said or felt, so I developed a really negative outlook. Then one morning I was arrested for I don't know what, so you can imagine how I felt. The Law—in fact the entire cosmos—seemed turned against me. Did somebody rat on me? Like who?

"At the trial I got a break one afternoon; the door-keeper said I could take a walk. I happened onto the Halbleibs' workshop and dropped in to see what it was all about.

"I was doubtful at first. But the Halbleibs showed me that the world looked bleak because I was coming from Hang Dog. Using the New Tricks I learned in this work-shop, I recalled a traumatic childhood incident: When I was six months old, my grandfather, who was incredibly nearsighted, mistook me for a leftover turkey and tried to have me for a midnight snack. My natural response was a lingering terror and a crippling fear of being salted. But my father just said, 'Good grief, Josef, get over it! Anyone could make a mistake like that.' Well, I say now, 'No, Papa—good grief is precisely what you denied me.'

"The Halbleibs allowed me to sob openly and rage

If you want to meet your needs,
you have to know what train they're on.

against their workshop pillows (available for a small materials fee). They convinced me that the only true Law is Inner Dog Law, *and I'm not guilty!*"

Josef K. subsequently got off on the Twinkie defense.

What Josef K. learned through our workshop was that his childhood anxieties were not his fault; they were the result of his father's cruelty to him. He learned that it's okay to be angry at your parents.

**Some say let sleeping dogs lie.
We say let awakened dogs speak truth.**

You may ask, as some critics have, If anger is okay for me, why wasn't it okay for my parents? Aren't they busy dealing with their own Inner Dogs? Weren't their parents mean to them, too?

Look, most of us have a lot invested in idealizing and protecting our parents. When we're kids, the thought that Mommy and Daddy might be flawed is terrifying; if they're fallible, who'll protect us, who's in charge? As adults, criticizing the folks feels like blaming, and is likely to trigger our puppyhood shame.

We say *making someone else responsible for our troubles is not blaming.*❖

When we get over idealizing our parents, we swing in the opposite direction. We say to ourselves, "I'm never going to be like them!" And then the next thing we know, we're listening to Mantovani, drinking martinis through a hose, and saying things to our own children like, "Knock it off or I'll turn this car around right now!" That's called Repetition Compulsion and it happens with all sorts of behaviors. That's called Repetition Compulsion and it happens with all sorts of behaviors.

Just because Mom was a bitch or Dad was a cur, that doesn't mean you're doomed. Most of us are, however, part of a dynasty of dysfunction, though perhaps not so venerable a one as that of a recent workshop participant, who shared the following:

"Hi, we are Elizabeth R. and we are a compulsive overcontroller. We are also powerless over pervasive doggie odor—in spite of the fact that we are, by the grace of God, Her Most Excellent Majesty, Ruler of the Realm, Head of the Commonwealth, and Defender of the Faith. But of course we can't tell you which Realm, Commonwealth, or Faith.

"Our family has been severely *farblundget* for generations. One of our ancestors was probably Jack the Ripper, and our father became king when our uncle abdicated to

❖For a more detailed explanation of this thesis, see our book *From Shame-based to Shane-based: Family, Blame, and the Archetype of the Surprisingly Short Lonesome Stranger.*

marry an American divorceé. They went into exile and eventually became a miniseries.

"We thought we'd escaped the family Love Curse. (We don't call having separate bedrooms for forty-five years a curse, do you?) But the marriages of our sister and three of our four children have all gone bad.

"We blamed ourself, until we took the Halbleibs' workshop and got in touch with our Inner Dog, a Welsh corgi called Lilibet. Now we see that we were the innocent victim of bungled uncling, and that our children and children-in-law are responsible for themselves. If they want to engage in extramarital toe sucking or be someone's feminine hygiene product, that's their problem. In fact the whole damned empire can go to hell for all we care!"

Non "Cave Canem" sed "Senti Canem."
(Not "Beware of the Dog"
but
"Be Aware of the Dog.")

NEW TRICKS

Sometimes a frightened, shamed Hang Dog acts out violently, as Mad Dog.✼ Learning to express anger forcefully but appropriately—being in your Angry Dog but not in your Mad Dog—is a crucial step in forgiving your parents.

You have our permission—no, our encouragement—to get in touch with your Mad Dog. It must be awakened in order to be put to sleep.

1. Ask Mad Dog why it's so angry. Make an Angry Dog Mask or an Angry Dog Pair of Pants. Wear them and do an Angry Dog Dance. Have fun making Angry Dog Sounds. Wear your Angry Dog Mask and your Angry Dog Pants to work, and then to the gym.

2. Very often, parents ask children questions but don't give them a chance to answer. Take a moment to think of the answers you would have given to the following questions, if you'd been allowed the opportunity.

🐾 Will you be happy when it's broken?

🐾 Who the hell do you think you are?

✼Other subspecies of Hang Dog are not covered in this book but will be handled in future volumes. These include Corn Dog (in whom early shame is transmuted into a compulsion to tell stupid jokes), Chili Dog (in whom sexual shame results in frigidity, impotence, and other disorders of desire), and Devil Dog (who experiences a form of demonic possession requiring no mere workshop but a full exorcism).

🐾 If Lylette Stanley jumped off a cliff, would you do that, too?

3. Write a letter from your Inner Dog to your parents, telling them everything you've ever wished you could say to them. If that's too painful, start by composing a similar letter that Emilio Estevez might write to Martin Sheen.

4. We the Halbleibs have discovered that in most families, people fall, or are pushed, into one of the following categories of Inner Dog troubles:

🐾 The Saint Bernard Syndrome: Obsessive rescuing; a Compassion Compulsion.

🐾 The One Hundred and One Dalmatians Syndrome: Sibling rivalry squared, plus one.

🐾 The Rin-Tin-Tin Syndrome: Tough, rigid, a good soldier—on the outside. On the inside: private grief, corporal punishment, major meshugas, general malaise.

🐾 The Goofy Syndrome: Your zany antics mask pain. Beneath that plastic barf is a breaking heart.

🐾 The Lady and the Tramp Syndrome: You wish that you could travel his way—but he (or she) is an inappropriate romantic partner. Again.

To identify your syndrome, find your symptoms on this simple-to-use chart.

WHAT KIND OF SICK PUP ARE YOU?

A Handy Diagnostic Chart

Do you have any of the following symptoms?

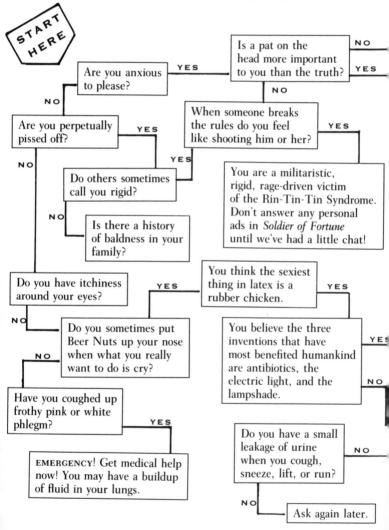

START HERE

Are you anxious to please? — **YES** →

Is a pat on the head more important to you than the truth? — **NO** / **YES**

NO ↓

Are you perpetually pissed off? — **YES** →

When someone breaks the rules do you feel like shooting him or her? — **YES** →

Do others sometimes call you rigid? — **YES** ↑

You are a militaristic, rigid, rage-driven victim of the Rin-Tin-Tin Syndrome. Don't answer any personal ads in *Soldier of Fortune* until we've had a little chat!

NO ↓

Is there a history of baldness in your family?

Do you have itchiness around your eyes? — **YES** →

You think the sexiest thing in latex is a rubber chicken. — **YES** →

NO ↓

Do you sometimes put Beer Nuts up your nose when what you really want to do is cry? — **NO**

You believe the three inventions that have most benefited humankind are antibiotics, the electric light, and the lampshade. — **YES** / **NO**

Have you coughed up frothy pink or white phlegm? — **YES** →

EMERGENCY! Get medical help now! You may have a buildup of fluid in your lungs.

Do you have a small leakage of urine when you cough, sneeze, lift, or run? — **NO**

NO → Ask again later.

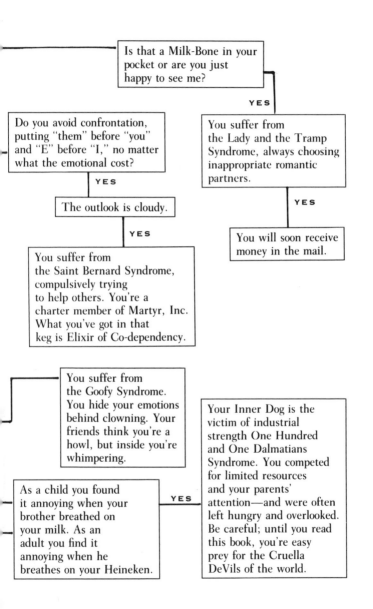

Is that a Milk-Bone in your pocket or are you just happy to see me?

YES

You suffer from the Lady and the Tramp Syndrome, always choosing inappropriate romantic partners.

YES

You will soon receive money in the mail.

Do you avoid confrontation, putting "them" before "you" and "E" before "I," no matter what the emotional cost?

YES

The outlook is cloudy.

YES

You suffer from the Saint Bernard Syndrome, compulsively trying to help others. You're a charter member of Martyr, Inc. What you've got in that keg is Elixir of Co-dependency.

You suffer from the Goofy Syndrome. You hide your emotions behind clowning. Your friends think you're a howl, but inside you're whimpering.

As a child you found it annoying when your brother breathed on your milk. As an adult you find it annoying when he breathes on your Heineken.

YES

Your Inner Dog is the victim of industrial strength One Hundred and One Dalmatians Syndrome. You competed for limited resources and your parents' attention—and were often left hungry and overlooked. Be careful; until you read this book, you're easy prey for the Cruella DeVils of the world.

THIS COULD HAPPEN TO YOU

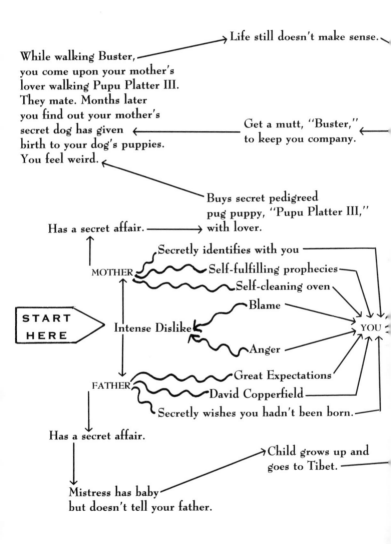

Life still doesn't make sense.

While walking Buster, you come upon your mother's lover walking Pupu Platter III. They mate. Months later you find out your mother's secret dog has given birth to your dog's puppies. You feel weird.

Get a mutt, "Buster," to keep you company.

Buys secret pedigreed pug puppy, "Pupu Platter III," with lover.

Has a secret affair.

MOTHER

Secretly identifies with you
Self-fulfilling prophecies
Self-cleaning oven
Blame

Intense Dislike

Anger

YOU

START HERE

FATHER

Great Expectations
David Copperfield
Secretly wishes you hadn't been born.

Has a secret affair.

Child grows up and goes to Tibet.

Mistress has baby but doesn't tell your father.

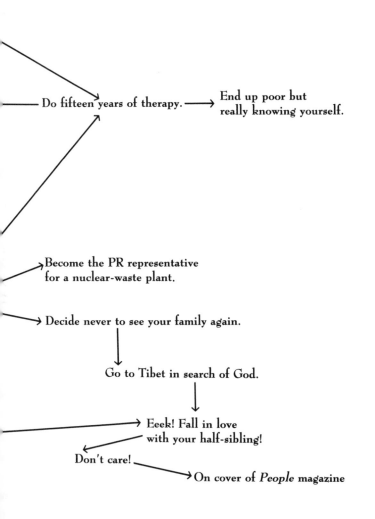

Do fifteen years of therapy. ⟶ End up poor but really knowing yourself.

Become the PR representative for a nuclear-waste plant.

Decide never to see your family again.

Go to Tibet in search of God.

Eeek! Fall in love with your half-sibling!

Don't care!

On cover of *People* magazine

LEFT
AT THE KENNEL

Issues of Abandonment

Don't make the mistake of assuming that you must actually have been abandoned to be haunted by Abandonment Issues. See if you recognize yourself in the statements below:

🐾 I'm disappointed when I don't get any mail.

🐾 When I lose a shirt button, I never believe I'll find another one that matches.

🐾 I'm still grieving over McLean Stevenson's leaving "M*A*S*H."

🐾 When I hear Vikki Carr sing, "Let it please be him,/ Oh, dear God, it must be him—but it's not him," that's when I die.

🐾 In fact, it seems as if everyone dies, sooner or later.

Did you respond "yes! absolutely!" or "nuh-uh, not me!" to any of these statements? We thought so.

If at any time during the crucial early development of your Wonder Dog, you were emotionally "left at the kennel"—that is, if your childhood needs went unattended or unacknowledged *even once*—you probably suffer from unresolved Abandonment Issues. They may manifest themselves in problems as diverse as stress acne, premature ejaculation, the inability to read maps, and serial murder.

Suppose, for example, that your mother left the infant you in a playpen. Frustrated and enraged by this imprisonment, you struggled to break out. But you were too tiny, too weak. Because of your mother's inattention to your needs ("But I had to make dinner!" she's likely to claim if you confront her today), you were unable to develop an Inner Dog with ego strength. You were robbed of the self-esteem that is the birthright of every child—and you still feel too wee and weak to burst free of psychic bonds. The only way you can physically manifest this desire for freedom is by "breaking out" in unsightly facial blemishes.

Let us put it bluntly: If you fail to retrain your Inner Dog, you'll always have an oily T-zone. You may even become one of those confused adults forced to use Retin-A and Oxy-10 at the same time.

Furthermore, if you were abandoned as a child, you are likely to expect abandonment in your adult life—no, to *invite* it.

On a first date you say such things as:

🐾 "I'm so sick and tired of unprotected sex!"

🐾 "Did you hear the fabulous quip that Rush Limbaugh made yesterday?"

🐾 "I've gone out with a lot of major babes."

🐾 "I've got two tickets to the Bruce Willis Film Festival."

At a job interview you announce to a potential employer:

🐾 "I've been fired from my last three jobs but I only sued twice."

🐾 "I hope my health insurance will cover drug counseling."

🐾 "What I really want is *your* job."

Or perhaps because you were abandoned you've become the abandoner. You leave lovers, jobs, unfinished symphonies. All are metaphors for the ultimate betrayal: You've deserted your Inner Dog, ignoring its pitiful howls, refusing to let it out to take a whiz. You've forgotten how to listen to yourself. You're denying your instincts.

How do you recover from abandonment and abandoning? Try the following:

NEW TRICKS

1. Affirmations against abandonment

Turn around three times and lie down on a comfortable mat. Imagine your adult self telling your Inner Dog:

- 🐾 You are the best dog in the world, and I'll never leave you, no matter what kind of mess you make.

- 🐾 It's okay to have a healthy interest in crotch sniffing.

- 🐾 I'm here to check you for ticks. You don't have to check me.

- 🐾 I'll love you even if you're mad, bad, and dangerous to know.

- 🐾 I'll love you even if you're nasty, brutish, and short.

- 🐾 I promise to consult you before I make any important decision. For example, if my boss offers me a promotion I will say, "It sounds like a good job but I have to ask my dog if it's okay."

2. Personal Beast
(check with your doctor or veterinarian before attempting the following exercise)

- 🐾 Get in touch with Mad Dog, roused from repression in chapter 4.

🐾 In a Mad Dog kind of voice say out loud just how rotten your life has been, how profoundly you've been betrayed by parents, siblings, friends, employers, therapists, and total strangers.

🐾 Place a towel between your teeth. Now growl, bark, pounce, shred, howl!🐾

🐾 Recall and relive the time your mother decided to go back to work after you were born. (So you were in college. Should that make a difference?)

🐾 Recall and relive the time your father wanted to watch the World Series instead of doing your homework for you.

🐾 Recall and relive the time your best friend got sick and wouldn't come out to play.

🐾 Recall and relive the shocking day Bob Dylan went electric.

🐾 Recall and relive your confusion when you learned that Lassie was a boy.

Now banish Mad Dog.

When you're drained of strength and emotion, you may want to lie on the floor quietly with a sock, a Pup-Peroni, or a Snausage-in-a-Blanket.

🐾 If the police or the city pound come knocking at your door, just tell them (politely) that this is therapy, that you're unleashing the beast— and best—within, and that they're welcome to participate.

3. *Letting go of resentments*

Pretend that you are torturing those who have wronged you. Imagine forcing them to watch a modern dance interpretation of Kathie Lee Gifford's autobiography. Imagine chopping them into pieces and mailing each piece to a different cable station.

Now forgive them!

Shihtzu happens.

HERA, THE DOG
THAT BIT YOU

Issues of Substance Abuse

In his epic/manifesto *Il Testosterone*, hairy guy and poet Robert Bly urges men to rediscover their "Zeus Energy." We, on the other hand, recommend rediscovering Hera, the Dog That Bit You. The best way for both sexes to recover from addiction is to get in touch with the Inner Dog.

We'll never forget the day in Los Angeles when Roger de B. shared his story!:

"I'm the only real recovering addict in the room," he began. The crowd stiffened.

"I'm an upholsterer." The room erupted in appreciative laughter.

"In fact, I'm a celebrity upholsterer. I can't tell you my clients' last names, but I can share that I did Cher's chairs. Maybe you've heard of my shop, Sofa's Choice? Or my new specialized boutique on Melrose, The Ottoman Empire?

"It's been a year since my first Inner Dog workshop—

and I'm not the same person. Let me tell you about the old me.

"Whatever you call my favorite piece of furniture—sofa, couch, chesterfield, divan, davenport, love seat—I've passed out on it. The movie of my life was produced by Darryl F. Xanax and directed by Jack Daniel, and it starred Sara Lee.

"Why? Because I was a lonely person. I'd spend my day fitting the stars for slipcovers, but who did I come home to? Workaholism couldn't cushion me from the sadness I felt, so I began drinking, drugging, and fooding.

"I didn't need a certified color counselor to tell me I was blue. But I needed the Halbleibs to tell me the problem was my Inner Dog.

"Before I met them I was so hungry for contact that—this is tough to admit—I used to go to restaurants and purposely choke on food so someone would give me a Heimlich hug.

"I wanted touch. I want to be petted. My Inner Dog needed attention, but I didn't know how to give it. I didn't know how to get close to anyone. I was in pain, and I was using substances to medicate myself."

When you find yourself at the intersection of Just Say No and Just Do It, do you consistently make a wrong turn?

The roots of that decision lie in your childhood. Let us tell you about some of the addicts we've worked with.

🐾 Barbara F. never got the Christmas presents she'd hinted for. It's not hard to see why she wound up being a heroin addict.

🐾 David K.'s mother insisted he eat dessert *after* dinner, not before. Naturally, he became a compulsive overeater and undertaker.

🐾 When William R. was a boy, his father wouldn't let him have the car on prom night. No wonder he became a compulsive gambler and eventually squandered the family fortune.

Beneath the addiction of all three was fear.

Beneath the fear was rage.

Beneath the rage was shame.

Beneath the shame was grief.

Beneath the grief was pain.

Beneath the pain was a ball of molten iron 700 miles in diameter.

And beneath that was the Inner Dog, waiting to be rescued.

No pain, no gain, no shoes, no shirt, no service.

The typical addict reacts to pain, rage, shame, and molten iron by becoming antisocial or, perhaps, compulsively social. Addicts are rebellious—or conformist—or they walk a middle road between the two. Some cover up an essentially sweet nature with nastiness. Just as often they cover up a nasty nature with sweetness. They can be angry at certain times and nice at other times, but not as angry or nice as they wish they'd been.

Recognize yourself?

We call such behavior "coming from your wound." Substance abuse is, of course, a misguided attempt to heal that wound. *Substance* can mean not only drugs and alcohol but also food, any brand of bottled water with an umlaut, automobile air fresheners shaped like pine trees, Brut, and weapons-grade plutonium.✻

Many people who are aware of substance abuse don't know about a common cross-addiction: intangibles abuse. For example, a person can be addicted to emotions. We're sure you know someone who's addicted to anger as an antidote to shame and fear. (Maybe this person isn't a full-service rageholic, but merely a whino.) Maybe a member of your family was a peevoholic, a trepidationoholic, an Itoldyousoholic, or a Mondaymorningquarterbackoholic.

Thought patterns can be addictive, too—living in your head, for example, or voting with your feet. So can china patterns, especially Wedgwood and Spode.

You might even be a fact addict. Here's how another workshop participant described such a problem:

"Hi, I'm Peter J. and I'm here because I'm an information junkie. I've absorbed so many facts that they show up

✻For more about the long history of addiction, see our book *Doing the Aztec Twelve-Step: Substance Abuse Among Ancient Meso-Americans.*

in urine tests. I've had to quit my job as a lathe operator so I can read all day and monitor CNN. I'm terrified that the one factoid I forget will be the one I desperately need someday. Suppose my future depends on knowing the obscure fact that a 1939 novel called *Gadsby* was written entirely without the letter *e*? My rational self sees that it isn't so important for me to know that Garibaldi buried his wife Anita on a beach (she was dead). But that tidbit from a high-school history book won't leave my head. It's just taking up space in my brain, and I'd like to leave room for something else, like memorizing the new U.S.D.A. "Eating Right" Food Pyramid. But there's always a chance, however slim, that a terrorist will take over a plane I'm riding on and announce, 'I will spare the life of anyone who can tell me where Garibaldi buried his wife.' A day at a time I'm trying to learn to live with such uncertainty."

If we are truly to lick our wounds, we must do so with the tongues of dogs and angels. Here are exercises that will help:

NEW TRICKS

1. Review the getting in touch with your Inner Dog exercise on page 22.
2. Get help from an Outer Dog.

The newly released and welcomed Inner Dog of an addict may be so confused at being substance-free that it doesn't know how to behave. Take as your role model an actual dog.

Savor every moment:
Bone appétit.

Until Inner Dog work comes naturally to you, you must act as if you have doglike qualities. We'd like to focus on one key area: canine ego strength.

Approach a dog—your own, that of a friend, relative, or trusted counselor, or one you encounter in the street. Lean over and make the following provocative statements:

🐾 "You're fired!" (Does the dog panic, cry, assume life is over, and run to the nearest bar?)

🐾 "Frankly, I find you sexually inadequate." (Does the dog burst into tears and run to the bathroom to do a line of coke?)

🐾 "You could lose a few pounds." (Does the dog growl at you, slink off to console itself secretly with a pint of peach ice cream, then stick its paw down its throat?)

🐾 "Your car's been towed." (Does the dog pitch a fit and OD on Ramlösa?)

We're willing to bet that all you get is a kind and quizzical look from the dog.

Mirror that look. Act "as if." Soon you'll handle life's ups and downs with the same strength, even in situations that formerly triggered drinking, drugging, fooding, other substancing, or intangibling.

HINT: At this delicate moment in your recovery, be wary of certain human emotions, especially worry, fear, happiness, despair, anxiety, anger, boredom, excitement, suspicion, confusion, indifference, elation, guilt, and disgust.

WHEN RETAIL
WAGS THE DOG

*Issues of Shopaholism
and Other Money Matters*

At nearly every Inner Dog gathering, we hear some variation of this story:

"Hi, my name is Monty R. III. I'm a caterer-metaphysican here in the Tri-City Area.

"I'm also a compulsive shopper.

"My problem began with the recession, when business slowed down. I didn't see what was happening at first, because I have so many other co-addictions and dis-eases.

"For one thing, I'm powerless over reruns of 'The Patty Duke Show' on Nick at Nite at 3:30 A.M. I told myself that I could stop any time—that I was just waiting for the episode where Patty and Cathy win a songwriting contest, and Jimmy Dean sings the song on TV, only Patty has plagiarized the lyrics, only it works out okay because the broadcast brings together the plagiarized poet and his long-lost love. Well, that show came and went and I was still watching.

"Around the time my unemployment ran out, I got hooked on the infomercial shows before and after 'Patty

Duke.' The more I worried about money, the more stuff I'd charge to my credit card. I certainly didn't *need* a Weed Whacker, a Garden Weasel, the Ronco Door Saver, the Popiel Pocket Pool Player, a *Slim Whitman: The Sun Sessions* boxed CD set, Mr. Microphone, Mr. Dentist, Mr. Enema, or the Splatter Screen.

"I thought I'd hit bottom, until the morning I was watching 'Rise and Shine Tri-City Area' and I saw that one of the other caterer-metaphysicians in town, my biggest competitor, in fact, was making up for lost business by charging five hundred dollars an hour to channel a fifty-thousand-year-old Neanderthal who gives party-planning advice. Why hadn't I come up with a gimmick like that? I was so depressed I immediately ordered a Snackmaster Dehydrator and a side of beef. I made so much jerky I was leaving it in my neighbors' mailboxes and unlocked cars. The more jerky I made, the less jerky I felt. But I was creating faux abundance; naturally, I crashed.

"By the time I caught the Halbleibs on 'Larry King Live,' I was desperately in debt and out of storage space. Then I heard them quote the famous Bavarian psychologist Baroness Braun und Krups von Hammacher-Schlemmer—"What for you need another tstotchka?" I hightailed it to a workshop."

The world is full of people like Monty. You may remember Alex, who was in the audience when we did an Inner Dog workshop on 'Oprah.' Last year he spent two thousand dollars a month on Big Gulps and other convenience store soft drinks because he got to keep the cup.❦

❦You'll find a detailed discussion of such incidents in our book *U-Totem and Taboo: Guilt, Shame, Shopping, and Convenience Stores.*

Or Portia, the compulsive car buyer whose Turtle Wax bills alone were sending her into bankruptcy.

Like Monty, Alex, and Portia, most compulsive shoppers have a closet or garage full of things but a heart full of empty. They seek protection from pain and grief behind a fortress of acquisitions. They feel powerless and helpless. They spend because they feel spent. They charge because they can't take charge. They're stuck in I-WANT-NESS, I NEED-NESS, I CAN'T-NESS, never able to get to I-HAVE-PLENTY-NESS, EVERYTHING-IS-OKAY-NESS, OR ELLIOT-NESS.

Monty, Alex, and Portia learned to recognize their problem and understand its cause. "I was shopping," Monty sobbed at his first workshop, "because I was afraid—afraid of failure, of success; of winning, of losing; of death, of life; of right, of left.

"I was shopping to avoid reviewing my options and taking risks. I was afraid of risks because I had no self-esteem. I had no self-esteem because my parents made me feel that I wasn't enough."

Once Portia understood her true motivations the epiphanies came fast and thick. "I saw that this particular *dis-ease* has to do with accumulating things that are too expensive. *Ex-pensive:* former thinking. I was trying to block out bad old thoughts." Specifically, Portia discovered that she shopped to block out the painful notion that her birth was a mistake. Her car compulsion had begun, she realized, the very day she learned she'd been accidentally conceived in the backseat of a Chevy.

"Note that *expensive* also contains the words *snipe*, *sieve*, *sex*, *vise*, *sin*, *envies*, and *penis*. I'm grateful to my Higher Power for sending me that insight," says Portia.

The word *environmental* has *iron men* hidden in it.

"I was searching for both acceptance from my mother and autonomy. Recently, I looked at the word *autonomy* as if for the first time. *Auto-no-my*. I got that I should take charge of my own transportation, sure, but maybe I shouldn't own a car. From now on I'll lease."

Sometimes the connection between shopping and pain is not so obvious. Take the case of Rudyard, who compulsively acquired faucet handles at hardware stores, auctions, and garage sales, or Janine, who hoarded fondue forks. At our workshops we teach shopaholics to look for the hidden metaphor. When Rudyard did so, he saw instantly that what he really wanted was to get a *handle* on things. Janine, who had cold, distant parents, was trying to create the *fond*ness she felt *due* her. And she felt she'd been well and truly *fork*ed.

Obvious or subtle, compulsive shoppers are coming from Hang Dog, and Hang Dog is coming from scarcity.

Hang Dog lives in deprivation, feeling there has never been enough love, attention, or comfort to go around. Buying is a misguided attempt to replace that missing love, attention, and comfort. In some extreme cases shopaholics aren't just trying to replace what they didn't get from their parents. They're trying to replace . . . themselves. We call that state of mind "coming from I-SHOULDN'T-HAVE-BEEN-BORN-NESS." Such people often consider themselves monsters. We call that "coming from LOCH-NESS."

Trying to reincarnate themselves ahead of schedule, they are perpetually shopping for a new wardrobe, new makeup, new home, new furniture, costly plastic surgery, and hair implants. Those who carry such behavior to an extreme often end up replacing all their internal organs.

Shopaholics swing between feeling that they deserve abundance and feeling that they deserve bupkes. Many end up in a cycle of bingeing and purging: Compulsive Shopping followed by Compulsive Returning. This compulsion can be tremendously embarrassing, especially when you're trying to return a liver, pancreas, or cornea.

We did come across one woman with an odd set of core issues. Pat had an unusual problem: periodically, she would order everything advertised in *The New Yorker*. Everything! The Tilley Hat, the Cunard Mozart Cruise, the Mont Blanc Meisterstück Hemingway Limited Edition Fountain Pen, the Lob-ster Tournament Model Ball Machine, the sterling silver Broccoli Pin.

"And the strange thing is," she told the group, "my sister Madge and my brother Sid are the same way."

We found the answer when Pat told us her real name.

It's Patchouli.

Her sister Madge was born "Magic." Sid is short for "Siddhartha."

They'd grown up on a commune; their parents were "hippies": attentive, loving, egalitarian, firm, but not shaming. They set loving limits but helped the children develop autonomy. They were as organic and nontoxic as parents can be, the model of a functional family.

The kids got lots of attention, but there wasn't much money. Furthermore, the parents were ideologically opposed to most popular toys. So for Christmas and birthdays there were no My Little Pony, no GI Joe, no Barbie's Carousel Kitchen, no Mattel Hot Wheels. They might get a hand-carved car, or a cornhusk doll, or a special outing, but no Nintendo, no Creepy Crawlers. Pat came to realize that she and her siblings were shopaholics *because they got love instead of the material things they so desperately craved.*

You know you're a shopaholic if you've ever:

🐾 Bought something you don't need.

🐾 Paid retail.

🐾 Bought something just to cheer yourself up.

🐾 Bought something without getting emotionally involved (Sport Shopping).

🐾 Bought something because there was only one left and it looked pathetic in the display all by itself (Mercy Shopping).

🐾 Owned a Clapper.

If you're a shopaholic, chances are you abuse money in other ways. Americans often confuse money with love, power, self-esteem.🐾 The now defunct commies were close (but didn't cop the stogie) when they called us Capitalist Running Dogs. We're Capitalist *Wounded* Dogs.

Mounting debt is the great American indoor sport. When the government owes fifteen trillion dollars, what's so bad about skipping a car payment? Members of Congress are nabbed for kiting checks. Norm on "Cheers" runs a tab for nearly ten years. Are we supposed to think debting is wrong?

Do you abuse your money? See if any of the following statements apply to you:

🐾 I use money several times a day.

🐾 I think about money at least once a day.

🐾 I need money.

🐾 When I have money, I feel good.

🐾 When I don't have money, I feel bad.

🐾Goodness knows we the Halbleibs have nothing against abundance in the form of money, consciously used and honestly acquired. Recovering compulsive underearners and overdressers ourselves, we now feel good about charging workshop participants three times what we did just one year ago.

🐾 I make more money now than I ever did—but I'd like more.

🐾 I stash money around the house.

🐾 I have more than one source of "income."

🐾 I hoard money in savings and money-market accounts.

Money abuse can be life-threatening in unexpected ways. One of the most extraordinary recovery experiences we ever witnessed transformed a young man who showed up without preregistering at a workshop in Bensonhurst, New York. He spent so much of the program nervously eyeing the exits we really didn't think he'd gotten much from the program. But when he finally shared, we were pleasantly surprised.

"Hi, I'm Vito 'the Cutlet' S.," he began intriguingly.

"Hi, Vito the Cutlet," the crowd responded with enthusiasm.

"I come from a dysfunctional and shame-based family: the Gambino family.

"Being the youngest son of a reputed crime boss isn't easy. I felt I never lived up to my father's expectations, and I certainly never got the nurturing I needed. I was given all the menial, boring chores nobody else wanted to do: breaking fingers, kneecapping, tasting sauce.

"My two older brothers had construction, hauling, and video arcades sewn up. So I decided to get into loan-sharking. I figured if I could get people to owe me money, lots of it, they'd have to be nice to me.

"I was so good at this racket that I got cocky. I didn't give the family a cut of the profits. Hey, I did this on my own! I thought my father would be proud, I'd be a made man. Instead, he put out a contract on me.

"I came into the Halbleibs' workshop to hide out. But I started to listen. I realized that I need to let my Inner Dog, Goombah, out to play every once in a while. I need to say 'Good dog, Goombah.' All along I was looking for approval and acceptance from my father and brothers when I really needed to give it to my Dog.

"I'm glad to be here. This program literally saved my life."

Vito the Cutlet, by the way, is now *Dr.* Vito the Cutlet; he's a psychotherapist who leads Made-Men's groups. These exercises helped him find personal fulfillment. We hope they'll do the same for you.

The dog who humps a table leg had better not mind splinters.

NEW TRICKS

1. Remember the portrait of your Inner Dog that you created in chapter 2? (If you haven't done so, do it now.) Place it in the credit-card section of your wallet. (If you've done a marble sculpture, you may need a shopping cart or wagon.)

Before you make a purchase at a store, look carefully at the portrait of your Inner Dog. Ask yourself, "Does my Inner Dog really need these items?" If not, resolve to meet its real needs—for food, a nap, a bath, a hug, some validation. Leave the items and walk away. Explain to the salesperson and any annoyed customers in line behind you, "Sorry, I changed my mind. My Dog needs nurturing, and *you* can't help."

2. Whenever you feel the desire to shop, ask yourself, "Is this a dog-based desire or a fear-based desire?" Feel your feelings. Are they rough, smooth, round, square, jagged, crenellated, crepuscular? Talk to your feelings. Say outloud, "Hello, Feelings. How are you today? Is there something you'd like to discuss?" Wait quietly until you get a response. By the time you do, the urge to shop will probably have passed.❦

❦What's coming up for you right now? Fear? Envy? Your lunch? It's not easy to confront your real feelings. You must feel your feelings, taste your tastings, smell your smellings.

Money talks, but you talk louder.

3. Money talks, but you talk louder. Take a dollar bill, raise it high over your head, and run around the house, office, or gym with it. Yell out, "Money is my friend."

Although we want you to feel comfortable with your money, we also want to make sure you know who has the upper hand. Place the dollar bill on the floor and shake your finger at it in an exaggerated fashion. Say to it sternly, "I'm the boss, you're nothing. You do whatever I tell you, and you go where I tell you. You may think you're going to the lingerie department at Bergdorf Goodman but in fact I'm sending you to the bank!" Practice until you can speak freely with your money.

HINT: Old nylon net makes a fabulous potato scrubber!

4. Recovery from debting begins with a repayment plan. Approaching creditors isn't easy because they're probably pretty angry by now. But if you explain that you're doing Inner Dog Work they may back off. Here is a sample correspondence:

> *Dear Mrs. Helmsley:*
>
> *We would like to advise you that your American Excrescence Card account is past due. Keeping your American Excrescence account in good standing is of the utmost importance. Our terms call for payment of the full balance on your American Excrescence Card account when you receive your statement; yadda yadda yadda take you to court, yadda yadda 10 days to respond, yadda yadda yadda.*
>
> > *Sincerely,*
>
> > *J. Miller*
> > *Account Services*
> > *American Excrescence, Inc.*

And here is a sample response:

> *To the Inner Dog of J. Miller*
> *Account Services*
> *American Excrescence, Inc.*
>
> *Dear J.:*
>
> *I know you intend to take me to court because I owe $10,000 for charges of clothing, jewelry, and a trip to the Caribbean, and I accept that. I need to say to you that my Inner Dog is committed to*

paying you back. But not right now, because it is in the process of facing its shame-based fear of worthlessness and failure. I know that as soon as I can fully own these feelings and incorporate them positively in my life, the universe will provide me with the abundance (money) to pay you back.

I am grateful for the increased awareness brought about by your bills, threatening notices, early morning phone calls, and orders to appear in court. And I forgive you.

J., the dog within me salutes the dog within you.

Sincerely,

SEE SPOT RUN

Issues of Workaholism

Workaholism was a disease that peaked in the eighties,[*] yet it persists to this day. There are still power-breakfasters, Filofaxophiles, disciples who await the return of Boesky and Milken, Gekkoites who believe that greed remains good.

You don't need an M.B.A. from Wharton to see that workaholics use their careers to avoid intimacy, compensate for feelings of inadequacy, and drone drone drone. What makes Spot run? Living in the fast lane, training for the rat race, and scaling the corporate ladder are pathetic attempts to compensate for an internal deficit. Greed is about need.

The form of workaholism we treat most often today is Post-it Traumatic Stress Disorder. Sufferers paper their walls, desk, lamp, chair, even their clothing, with sticky-

---

[*] So many people have been laid off recently that it threatens to be replaced by outofworkaholism.

backed slips of paper marked with lists, reminders, and phone numbers that seem to have hieroglyphic significance to them.

The fast track is great for the greyhound. But what of the basset?

Our cure for workaholism, eighties or nineties variety, is simple:

Work like a dog.

We mean:

🐾 Work without attachment to results.

🐾 Do one thing at a time. (A dog sticks to the matter at paw. If she's pulling a sled, she's pulling a sled, not simultaneously creating a marketing plan for tartar-control, beef-basted Chew-eez.)

🐾 Stop comparing yourself to others.

🐾 Respond honestly:

> When you itch, scratch.
> When you're tired, sleep.
> When you're hungry, eat.
> When you're enthusiastic, wriggle.

When you itch, scratch.

NEW TRICK

Sometimes workaholism is the result of not being in the right job. Take this brief vocational quiz, modified from our best-seller *What Color Is Your Garbage Chute?*

I'd rather work indoors than outdoors.

———— YES ———— NO

I'd rather work alone than in a group.

———— YES ———— NO

I'd rather be top dog than just one of the pack.

———— YES ———— NO

I'd rather be a big fish in a small pond than a small fish in a big pond.

———— YES ———— NO

I'd rather be a hammer than a nail.

———— YES ———— NO

I'd rather be a sparrow than a snail.

———— YES ———— NO

I'd rather see you dead, little girl, than to catch you with another man.

———— YES ———— NO

I'd rather be blue thinking of you than be happy with somebody else.

———— YES ———— NO

There is no place else on earth that I would rather be.

———— YES ———— NO

Two of our clients profited mightily from taking this inventory. Colleagues at Morgan Stanley, they were terrifically unhappy in their work. After getting in touch with their Inner Dogs at our popular Wall Street center, they realized that what they really wanted was to head their own rap groups. You know them today as LL Bean Cool J and 2 Live J. Crew.

Work like a dog.

A SCARY
NEW HYBRID

Issues of Workshopaholism

Although we don't see as many active shopaholics and workaholics as we used to—a lot of them are in recovery, like the economy—more and more often, we're encountering an alarming new hybrid: the workshopaholic, powerless over support groups, programs, adult-education classes, symposia.

We recently treated a woman who in one week attended Mañana, the procrastinator's support group; the Grassy Knoll Institute for Zapruder Mind Method (a frame-by-frame meditative study of the Kennedy assassination film); a Postmenopausal Zest Confab; and a Manifesting Inner Light practicum. She did Avatar Work, Sand Play, Postural Integration, the Feldenkrais Method, Aikido, Sunrise-Circle work, a tour of power vortices in Sedona, Arizona, and the annual meeting of Womanose: Intuitive Knowledge Through Aromics. She participated in a How-to-Extend-Your-Orgasm-Until-a-Year-from-Shavuous workshop, a Healing Crystals workshop, and a Folgers Crystals workshop.

On the way to our Inner Dog workshop, she stopped at a meeting of a support-group abuser's support group.

Later, she made a particularly ugly revelation that bodes ill for the future: She has, she told us, sued several workshop leaders because she found the enlightenment acquired under their guidance to be transitory or inadequate. And she knows several other workshopaholics who've filed similar suits.

We helped her see that her litigiousness masks pain, and that she'll never get the results she seeks until she fully knows and loves her Inner Dog. But just in case, we've retained as counsel the prestigious firm of Lather, Rinse, and Repeat, which specializes in workshop malpractice.

There is no word that rhymes with *husband*.

SEXUAL HEELING

Issues of Intimacy and Commitment

🐾 Larry always seems to choose women who end up leaving him for top-ranking officials of the PLO.

🐾 Ginger consistently falls for men who collect antique tractor seats.

🐾 Jeannie is in love with a married man. Her father.

As these examples clearly show, unresolved Inner Dog issues are responsible for a whole range of relationship troubles, including fear of intimacy, ambivalence about intimacy, fear of ambivalence about intimacy, intimacy addiction, and abuse of the words *intimacy* and *addiction*.

Workshop participants and talk-show audiences ask us more questions about love and intimacy than about any other subject. Here are some Qs we get over and over—and our As:

Q. Exactly how do I get my Inner Dog involved in the dating process?

A. Get into the practice of consulting your Inner Dog at every step of the way. Start with saying to a prospective date, "I'd love to go out with you, but let me check with my Inner Dog." (Such statements also help weed out people who don't accept who you truly are.) Later in the relationship please don't forget that safe sex starts with an Inner Dog consultation. If your date makes a move, say, "Wait!

' "Wait! Before you kiss me I'd like to se

Before you kiss me I'd like to see if my Inner Dog feels comfortable right now." We know one woman who gave her Inner Dog the name Trojan as a gentle reminder.

Q. How come the opposite sex treats me like dirt?

A. Maybe you give them grounds! But all seriousness aside, are you sure you aren't coming from Hang Dog? You teach your mate how to treat you by how you treat yourself.

if my Inner Dog feels comfortable right now."

Have you ever said something like, "No, don't pick me up. I'll meet you at the restaurant. I'll be coming directly from my shame"?

There's healthy, honest shame, of course—the shame we feel when we admit to liking "Married . . . With Children," or the shame we feel when we can't remember whether Lawrence Welk is dead or alive.

But then there's the unhealthy shame we feel for just being who we are. And this gets transmitted to our romantic partner, as if we wore a giant computerized sign that says "Kick me!" How do you change the message on the sign? Take care of your Inner Dog!

Q. My mate says I don't contribute my share to the relationship, emotionally, financially, or practically. Is that bad?

A. Congratulations! A healthy relationship involves risk. One of the more frightening risks is, of course, letting someone take care of you. We admire your courage in letting him or her do more of the housework, bring in more family income, initiate sex more often. How else will you kick the caretaking habit? Caretakers are secret control freaks. Bravo for breaking the cycle.

Q. Where can I find intimacy?

A. See Figs. 1–3.

Q. I've always been someone's daughter, lover, wife, mother, sister, tree surgeon, Navy SEALs commando. How do I know when I'm doing something because I want to and when I'm doing it to please others? I really can't tell anymore!

A. It's hard to know these days when you're following your instincts and when you're being swayed by societal or family pressure—that is, when you're coming from your

THE THREE FIGS
OF INTIMACY

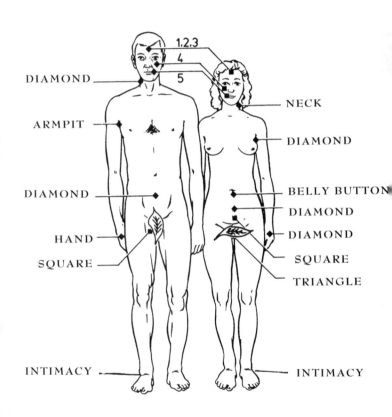

DIAMOND

ARMPIT

DIAMOND

HAND

SQUARE

1,2,3

4

5

NECK

DIAMOND

BELLY BUTTON

DIAMOND

DIAMOND

SQUARE

TRIANGLE

INTIMACY

INTIMACY

FIG. **1**

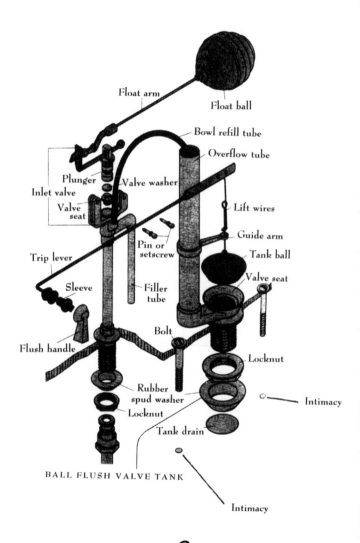

Float arm

Float ball

Bowl refill tube

Overflow tube

Plunger

Valve washer

Inlet valve

Valve seat

Lift wires

Pin or setscrew

Guide arm

Tank ball

Trip lever

Valve seat

Sleeve

Filler tube

Flush handle

Bolt

Locknut

Rubber spud washer

Intimacy

Locknut

Tank drain

BALL FLUSH VALVE TANK

Intimacy

FIG. 2

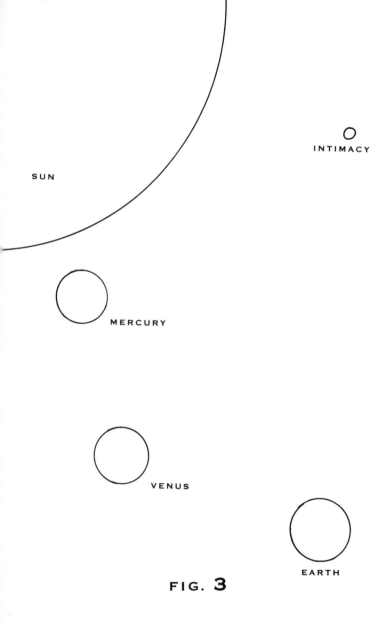

SUN

INTIMACY

MERCURY

VENUS

EARTH

FIG. **3**

Inner Dog and when you're *not* coming from your Inner Dog. Is that your gut talking, or is it a replay of parental tapes, or are you the victim of subliminal ATTEND OUR WORKSHOP advertising? The only way to know for sure is to engage in a dialogue—preferably written—with your Inner Dog. While this can be intrusive in some situations—in a bank line, say, or in bed—Dog Work is the only surefire guide.

Detach and save.

EXTRA CREDIT ESSAY QUESTION:
Is using a dictionary denying your instincts? Should you come from your Dog and go with what you feel a word *ought* to mean? Or is it more productive to bow to convention in this case?

Q. Can you suggest some healthy love play?

A. We suggest Red Rover, Red Rover for groups. For an intimate tête-à-tête, why not a tug-of-war for two? If you're new to this activity, don't try it except under a therapist's supervision.

We get many, many inquiries about how to improve communication in a marriage or live-in relationship. Here's our favorite tip.

NEW TRICK

Communicate anger in healthy ways. Baring your teeth and barking are fine in a workshop setting, but they may be counterproductive at home—for example, when your lover tells you he or she forgot to make your coffee in the morning.

Try saying this: "What's true for me today is that I have angry feelings concerning what I heard you say when you said what you said. It reminds me of what my mother said when she said what she said, and that hurts me and so that's where I'm at with this, and it's not all right with me for today." This should help to avoid a lot of communication problems.

BONUS: Here's a new twelve-step program to improve your partnering skills.

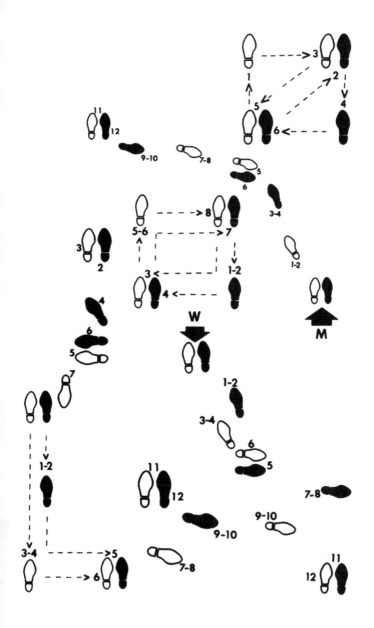

THE TWELVE-STEP
INNER DOG RECOVERY PROGRAM

1. Step forward on left foot.
2. Move to side on right foot,
   remembering to "brush" the left ankle.
3. With left hand at waist level
   and thumb on back of partner's right hand,
   step to the side on left foot.
4. Rock back on ball of left foot.
5. Replace weight on right foot.
6. With right knee slightly bent,
   take small step back on flat of right foot,
   transferring weight and straightening leg
   until "sitting" on right hip.
7. Beginning with the left foot,
   take six steps backward clockwise,
   covering approximately a half circle.
8. Close right foot to left foot,
   continuing to lead current partner across.
9. Cha-cha-cha diagonally forward to right.
10. Step forward on left foot with thighs locked,
    right shoulder and hip in advance of left.
11. Hop on left foot.
12. Turn to face partner in closed position.

If you're new to this activity,
don't try it except under a therapist's supervision.

12

YOUR GARAGE

Issues of National Geographic

Lots of old ones, in dusty stacks.

Get rid of them—now.
Or cherish them forever.
Your Inner Dog will know what to do.

BIG ARNOLD
AND LITTLE ARNOLD

Famous People and Their Inner Dogs

New scholarly findings constantly suggest that geniuses in other ages and disciplines have flirted with Inner Dog theory.

Art historians tell us that before Michelangelo completed his awesome *David* he practiced by sculpting his dog, coincidentally also named David, in a similar pose. Michelangelo wrote about David (the dog, not the biblical king) in a letter to a close friend:

"You know, *I think we're a lot alike*, me and David (the dog, not the biblical king)." (Italics ours.)

Among the papers of Samuel Beckett, currently being catalogued at Bob Jones University, scholars have discovered what appears to be a previously unknown first draft of *Waiting for Godot*, portentously entitled *Waiting for Dogot*.

Reconstructionist critics at the southern college insist that the title is a typo. But We the Halbleibs recognize it for what it really is: The play resembles nothing so much as an Inner Dog dialogue! But you be the judge, based on this excerpt:

SB: Hi. I'd like to get to know you. Would you like to get to know me?

MUTTT: There is nothing to express, nothing with which to express, nothing from which to express, no power to express, no desire to express, together with the obligation to express.

SB: I take that as a *yes*. What do you enjoy doing?

MUTTT: Nothing to be done.

SB: Well, sure, there's lots to be done. What do most Inner Dogs like to do?

MUTTT: They give birth astride a grave, the light gleams an instant, then it's night once more.

SB: Does that mean you'd like me to scratch your tummy?

We think that Beckett may have hit upon Inner Dog theory before we did. (That's nothing to be ashamed of; gunpowder was invented simultaneously on three continents.) We believe this tentative first encounter with his Inner Dog, Muttt, was so profoundly painful that Beckett, by all accounts a cheerful fellow up to this point, became the gloomiest of Guses and completely changed his style and themes.

Other writers have left evidence of forays into Inner Dogdom. Virginia Woolf's novel *Flush* was a fanciful biography of Elizabeth Barrett Browning's spaniel. Woolf's own biographer, her nephew Quentin Bell, writes, "*Flush* is not so much a book by a dog lover as a book by someone *who would love to be a dog.*" (Italics formerly ours but recently optioned by Steven Spielberg.)

And need we say more about Dylan Thomas's contribution than its title, *Portrait of the Artist as a Young Dog*?

One scholar has spent years trying to prove that

Proust's madeleine was not a small cake but a favorite poodle that was inexplicably tortured by Proust's aunt. *Swann's Way*, this scholar believes, is actually a highly symbolic account of Proust's anguish at watching helplessly as his aunt dipped poor Madeleine's paws in scalding lime-flower tea every Sunday. Fascinating.

We have our suspicions about other historical personages, but we'll never know for sure. (Although a client who channeled during a workshop was able to tell us that Hamlet's melancholy sprang from the fact that his Inner Dog was a good Dane but not a Great Dane.)

Hamlet: Not a Great Dane but a good Dane.

Michelangelo's *David*.

Another figure not usually associated with Inner Dog Work unexpectedly gave us a great deal of insight.

Before Joseph Campbell's death in 1987, Bill Moyers spent a summer with the mythology maven filming the interviews that would become the acclaimed PBS series "The Power of Myth." These meetings took place at the rustic Northern California cinema center that Julia Roberts built with the millions she made from *Pretty Woman*—beautiful Streetwalker Ranch.

"Ich bin ein Berliner."
—JFK

"Ich bin ein Weimaraner."
—JFK's Inner Dog

What few people know is that We the Halbleibs were able to grab a few afternoons with Campbell while Moyers was away filming a cameo appearance on "The Love Boat." Though we didn't realize it at the time, this discussion planted in our unconscious the seed that would later bloom dramatically into Inner Dog Theory.

Campbell mentioned to us that the dog probably joined the human family in 15,000 B.C., during the late Paleolithic era. He noted that there are dog archetypes in every culture: The Egyptians worshipped Anubis, jackal-headed God of the Dead. In Greek mythology the underworld was guarded by the three-headed watchdog Cerberus. (His three-headed watch showed the time in Athens, New York, and Tokyo.) When an Aztec died, a red-haired dog was killed and cremated with the deceased in order to carry him across the river of the underworld. According to the Aranda tribe of Australia, certain cave spirits are visible only to dogs and holy people. And some Americans still worship Benji, God of Elevated Blood-Sugar Levels. Come to think of it, though, Campbell never said word one about his Inner Dog.

What he really wanted to talk about was his plan to create with Moyers a new series of videos, a project that was, unfortunately, preempted by Campbell's own trip on the back of a red-haired dog.

We will always mourn what might have been. But Campbell did give us a copy of the prospectus and marketing plan for the video series. We'd like to share them with you:

BILL MOYERS
AND JOSEPH CAMPBELL:
THE LOST EPISODES

🐾 *The Power of Myth Workout:* The Seven Labors of Hercules were nothing compared to the workout Joseph Campbell and Bill Moyers have planned for you. Move over Jane and Jake! Not even Richard Simmons's "Schvitz to the Hitz" can match the intensity of this offering from pecs' bad boy.

♿ *Follow Your Blintz:* Joseph Campbell on Jewish cooking.

♿ *Where the Fore! Winds Blow:* Using myth to improve your golf swing.

♿ *Hero with a Thousand Farces: The After-dinner Speaker's Guide to Humor of the Ancient World.* Includes the step-by-step instructions for successfully pulling off Campbell's famous bit that begins, "A priest, a rabbi, and a shaman are in a lifeboat . . ."

We've launched two interesting, long-term studies on celebrities and their Inner Dogs. In one we'll be examining whether the names of famous people influence their relationships with their Inner Dogs. We'll be working with Joe Cocker, Cybill Shepherd, and Mark Spitz. We'll also examine how a person's profession affects his or her image of the Inner Dog. Does Muhammad Ali look within and see a boxer, for example, or Julia Child a chow, or Madonna a whippet?

We never reveal the full names of our more celebrated clients without getting their permission first. So rest assured that Cocker, Shepherd, and Spitz know they're mentioned in this book.

And rest assured that Arnold Schwarzenegger is fully aware that we're discussing his relationship with his Inner Dog, a miniature schnauzer he calls Little Arnold. (We want to eat lunch in this town again!)

Arnold first met Little Arnold when he was competing for the title of Mr. Universe. Intuitively foreshadowing the Inner Dog Movement, he would visualize the feisty dog as a reminder to work harder. Obviously, the image worked. And today Little Arnold accompanies Big Arnold to negotiations for movie deals. It is rumored that Arnold sometimes excuses himself briefly from meetings when the pressure mounts. We know why: Big Arnold has gone off to a quiet place to play with Little Arnold.

EXTRA CREDIT:

Arnold Schwarzenegger's miniature schnauzer
and its psychosocial implications
for twentieth-century cinema: Discuss.

14

A FINAL WORD

Carry this book with you. Refer to it in times of crises. And when in doubt, remember . . .

Don't just do something—*dog* something.